Dancing for God

Written By Ali Timmer   Illustrated By Makayla Roe

This is a work of fiction.

Paperback ISBN: 979-8-9914491-6-8

To all Christians living for His glory
-A.T.

And whatever you do, whether in word or deed, do it all in the name of the Lord Jesus, giving thanks to God the Father through him.
-Colossians 3:17

In a town much like yours, with shops, families, and friends, lived Abby. Abby was just like her neighbors, expect she was a Christian and was homeschooled.

Abby dreamed of becoming a ballerina since the day she watched her sister, Sarah, dance on stage. Sarah danced a solo as Clara. Abby thought that maybe *one day she be as good as Sarah. Maybe she could even have a solo and be the star!*

Before Abby could have a solo, she needed to learn how to dance. Today was her chance. Mommy was taking her to her new ballet class at Verity Ballet. Abby excitedly watched the clock, waiting in her leotard, for Mommy to say "Time to go!"

In class, Abby danced to her favorite songs from princess movies. Her favorite part was when she got to take her turn leaping across the floor. It was almost like being a star and having a solo!

Welcome to
Verify
Ballet

When class was over, Mommy walked in with Abby's sulking little brother, James. He got into bad moods a lot. Abby wondered what it was about now.

Ms. Hannah

Mr. Noa

"How was ballet?" Mommy asked.

"It was good!" Abby replied.

"Almost my whole class is homeschooled just like me! My teachers are Mrs. Hannah and Mr. Noah. Mrs. Hannah knows everything about ballet and Mr. Noah is so funny!"

"Oh, and at the end of the year, we're going to do a ballet about creation. It'll be fun! I've never been in a ballet about the Bible.

It's called the 'Colors Of Creation' and every day of the Creation story has a different color!" exclaimed Abby. *And maybe*, she thought, *I can have a solo and be the star, just like Sarah did!*

James started whining. "What about me? I be in the dance?"

"Not this time," said Mommy. "But we can cheer on Abby! Abby," she added, "I'm glad that you enjoyed your first day at Verity Ballet."

That night, as Abby fell asleep, she imagined the performance. She smiled. In her dream, she was dancing a solo part, just like Sarah.

Abby twirled,

leapt,

plièd,

and bowed.

I wonder what solo I'll get?
Abby thought as she brushed her teeth the next morning.

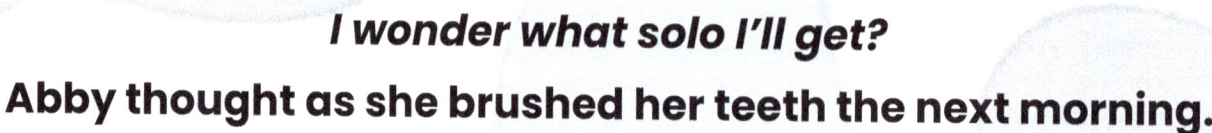

"Because." Abby put her toothbrush back in its spot, "Ballet is about getting a solo, just like Sarah. If you don't get a solo in ballet, it means you're a bad ballerina."

All week, Abby wondered what solo she would get. Would she be the sea?

Would she be the grass, with a green leotard and beautiful choreography made just for her?

She would be on stage alone. After all, getting a solo was what being a ballerina was all about.

"All right, class!" Mrs. Hannah called at her next class. "The Colors Of Creation tryouts are next week. Each color has a different dance for every day of the creation story." Abby smiled. It was almost time to get her solo.

For family worship that evening, Daddy read the creation story, Genesis chapter 1 and 2 from the Bible.

"On Day one, God separated the light from the darkness and made Heaven," Daddy read.

"On Day two, He gathered up the waters and made dry land and vegetation."

"On Day three He made the sun and the moon."

"On Day four, God made water and air animals."

"On Day five, God made land animals."

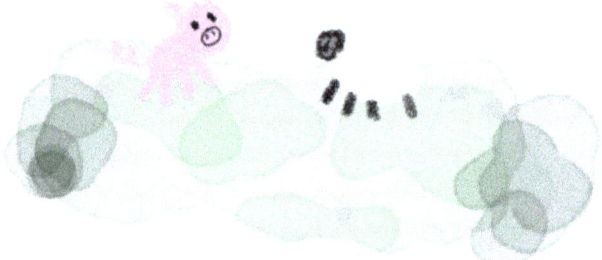

"On Day six He made man."

And on Day seven," "He rested!" cried James.

Daddy laughed. "Yes, He did and now it's time for bed. Besides, tomorrow's Abby's tryouts!" As Abby walked into her room, she remembered her father's word's with a shiver of excitement. Tomorrow she would get her solo, just like Sarah had.

The day of tryouts arrived. Abby danced, twirled, and leaped. She pointed her toes and followed the choreography. She knew with all her heart she would get a solo in the ballet. Now she just had to wait.

The next week at Verity, the cast for Colors of Creation was announced. Mrs. Hannah's voice raised above the clamor of the class. The room went quiet.

"I'm going to announce the cast for the Colors Of Creation Ballet! Everyone gets a part they're just not all the same. Remember, the important thing is you're dancing for God's glory."

Mrs. Hannah announced the different parts. There was a part for light, dark, fruit, man, animals, and the sun. Finally, Abby heard her name. "Abby and Lilly are going to be our blue sea," said Mrs. Hannah.

"How was it, Abby?" Daddy asked after class. Abby said, "Bad. I didn't get a solo!" Daddy replied, "Abby, you can still dance for God's glory even if you didn't get a solo." Abby sighed. Maybe Daddy was right, but without a solo, she knew she could never be as good as Sarah.

At bedtime, Sarah and Joel, read her the creation story.

"How was ballet?" Joel asked, after the story. "It was bad because I didn't get a solo." Abby sighed. "You don't need a solo," said Sarah. "Ballet is about dancing for God, just like everything we do." Abby frowned. Daddy had said that too. What was wrong with everyone?

Abby went to Verity every
week that year.

Mr. Noah taught the choreography for their sea dance.
Mrs. Hannah showed them their costumes and taught
them how to enter and exit the stage. Abby enjoyed her
time with Lilly, but inside, Abby was still mad about not
getting a solo.

Sarah, Joel and even grumpy James cheered, and helped Abby practice at home. Abby thought about what Sarah said about a solo , but she didn't believe it. Being good at ballet meant getting a solo.

Backstage, the dancers were getting ready. But Abby was upset. She didn't have a solo part, and now, she knew she would never be as good as Sarah.

"What's wrong, Abby?" asked Mrs. Hannah.
"I wanted a solo part!" cried Abby. Mrs. Hannah sighed.
"Ballet is about dancing for the glory of God, not getting
a solo." Abby thought for a moment. If Sarah and Mrs.
Hannah and Daddy all said the same thing, then they
must be right.

Abby nodded. Maybe Mrs. Hannah was right.
"Are you ready, Abby?" Lilly asked.   Abby nodded.
"Now I am." And she was. She was ready to dance
the Creation story for God's glory.

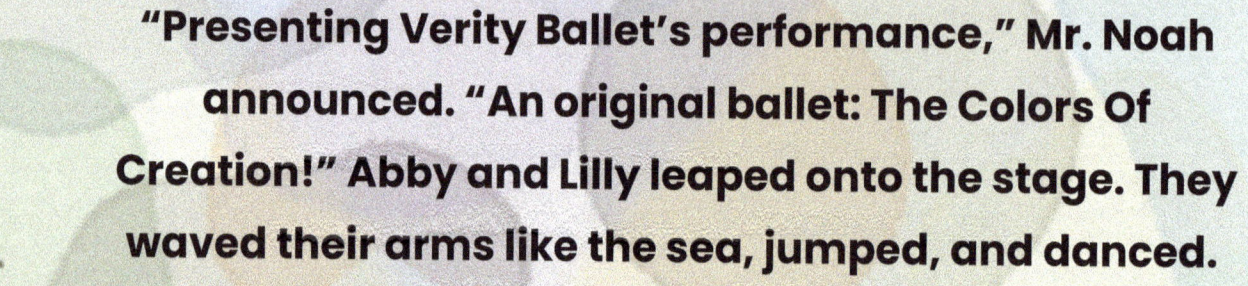

"Presenting Verity Ballet's performance," Mr. Noah announced. "An original ballet: The Colors Of Creation!" Abby and Lilly leaped onto the stage. They waved their arms like the sea, jumped, and danced.

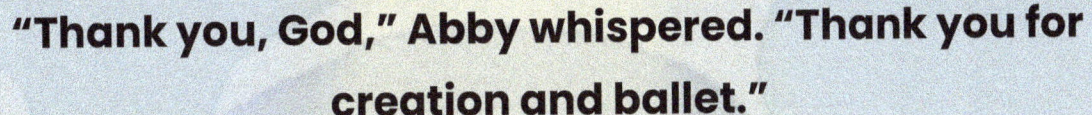

"Thank you, God," Abby whispered. "Thank you for creation and ballet."

Happiness filled Abby. She knew she was dancing for God even if she didn't get a solo. Maybe she wasn't as good as Sarah, but she could still dance for God. "I'm glad," she said to Lilly as they bowed, "I can dance for God and be the ballerina of the town!"

About The Makers

Ali Timmer

Ali Timmer is a teenage writer and homeschooler. Her favorite books include Anne Of Green Gables and the Wingfeather Saga. Her dream is to be a published author, wife, and mother. You can find her dreaming up new characters, playing soccer, or writing her blog; http://www.sagasandstories.wordpress.com/

Makayla Roe

Makayla Roe is a high schooler who is illustrating her story one day at a time. She is an Eagle Scout and Thespian, a proud member of her high school choir, and a writer and artist. She plans currently to go into either music/theater, art, or history, hoping to one day work at Silver Dollar City and make people smile while doing what she loves most.

Note for Parents

We all know how hard it is to raise our children to know God and to follow His word. In a culture that is inundated with excelling in sports we often forget that we should be participating for God's glory not our own. Our hope is that this book will help you guide your child to compete for God's glory and to focus on Him in every aspect of life.

The creation story can be found in Genesis 1 and 2. If you are looking for more resources on teaching your children Biblical truth, please check out
www.redeemingfamilypress.com
www.redeemingfamily.com

Creation Devotional

Little Pig on the Farm

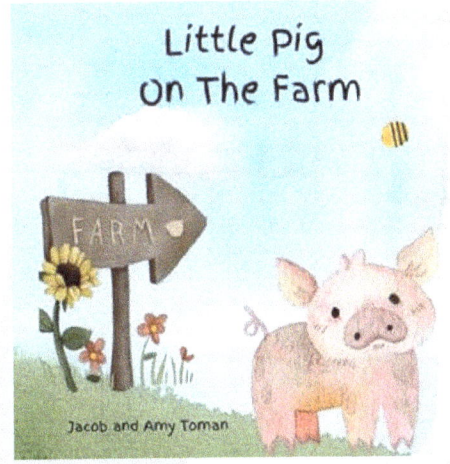

A Year Is

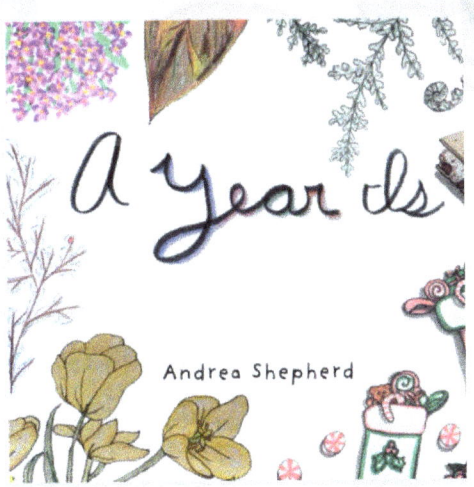

The Legend of the Donkey Knight

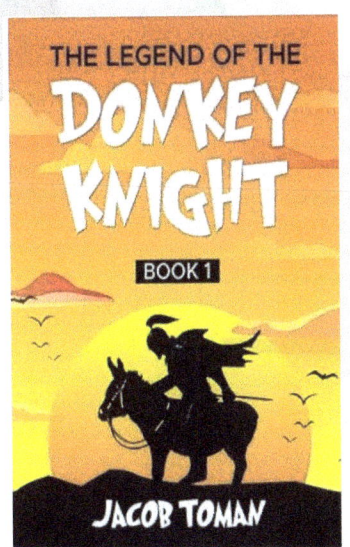